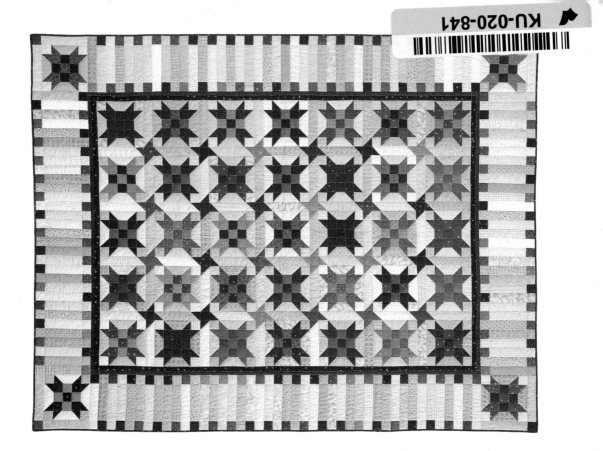

Farmer's Daughter, 75" x 96", © Country Threads, 1991.
Quilted by Elnora M. Paulson.

That Patchwork Place • PO Box 118 • Bothell, WA 98041-0118

*From **Country Threads** by Mary Tendall and Connie Tesene*

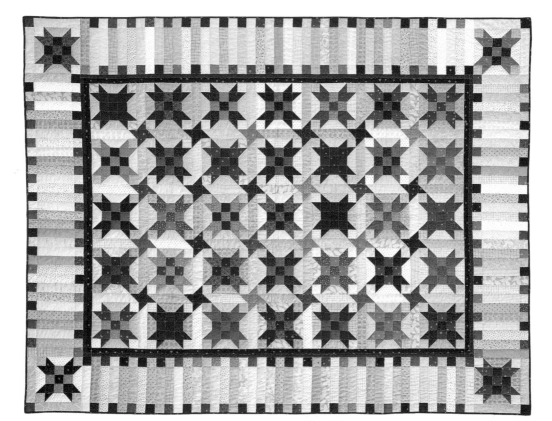

Farmer's Daughter, 75" x 96", © Country Threads, 1991.
Quilted by Elnora M. Paulson.

That Patchwork Place • PO Box 118 • Bothell, WA 98041-0118

*From **Country Threads** by Mary Tendall and Connie Tesene*

Is this Heaven? … No, It's Iowa in Summer, 27" x 37",
© Country Threads, 1991. Quilted by Gladys Jurgemeyer.

That Patchwork Place • PO Box 118 • Bothell, WA 98041-0118

*From **Country Threads** by Mary Tendall and Connie Tesene*

Is this Heaven? … No, It's Iowa in Summer, 27" x 37",
© Country Threads, 1991. Quilted by Gladys Jurgemeyer.

That Patchwork Place • PO Box 118 • Bothell, WA 98041-0118

*From **Country Threads** by Mary Tendall and Connie Tesene*

Massachusetts Cross and Crown, 65" x 76",
© Marsha McCloskey, 1991. Quilted by Virginia Lauth.

That Patchwork Place • PO Box 118 • Bothell, WA 98041-0118

*From **On to Square Two** by Marsha McCloskey*

Massachusetts Cross and Crown, 65" x 76",
© Marsha McCloskey, 1991. Quilted by Virginia Lauth.

That Patchwork Place • PO Box 118 • Bothell, WA 98041-0118

*From **On to Square Two** by Marsha McCloskey*

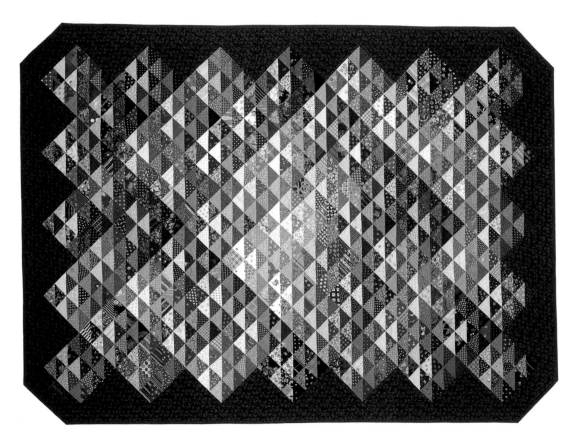

Charmed, I'm Sure, 58" x 78½",
©Judy Dafoe Hopkins, 1987.

That Patchwork Place • PO Box 118 • Bothell, WA 98041-0118

From **Rotary Roundup** *by Judy Hopkins and Nancy J. Martin*

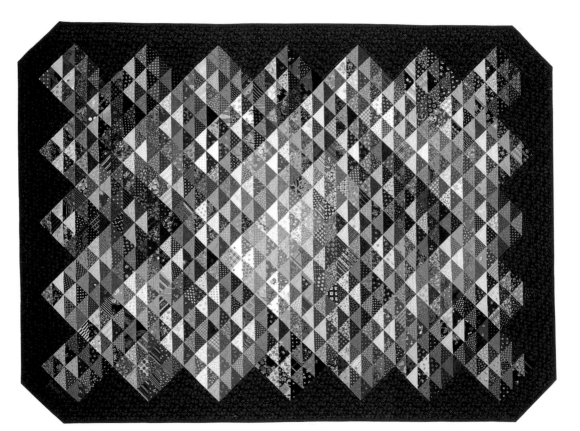

Charmed, I'm Sure, 58" x 78½",
©Judy Dafoe Hopkins, 1987.

That Patchwork Place • PO Box 118 • Bothell, WA 98041-0118

*From **Rotary Roundup** by Judy Hopkins and Nancy J. Martin*

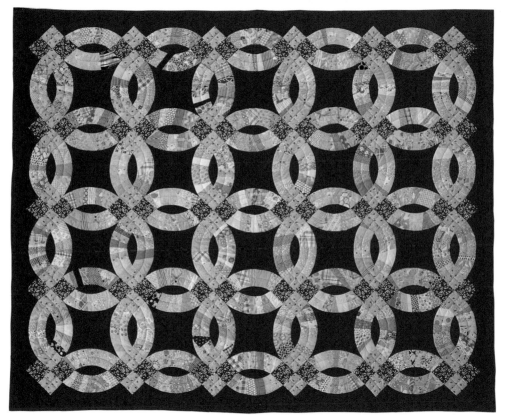

Double Wedding Ring, 70" x 82", © Bessie Sawyer Newman and Sharon Hicks Newman (started 1928, completed 1993).

That Patchwork Place • PO Box 118 • Bothell, WA 98041-0118

*From **Treasures from Yesteryear, Book One** by Sharon Newman*

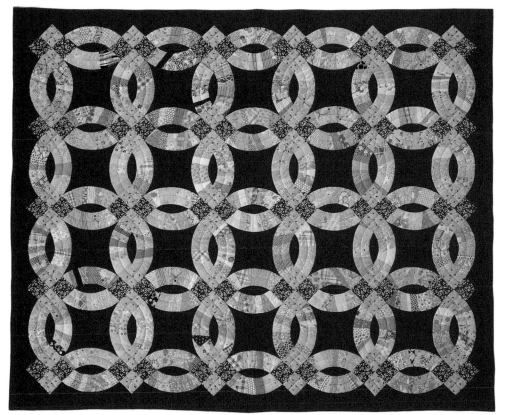

Double Wedding Ring, 70" x 82", © Bessie Sawyer Newman
and Sharon Hicks Newman (started 1928, completed 1993).

That Patchwork Place • PO Box 118 • Bothell, WA 98041-0118

*From **Treasures from Yesteryear, Book One** by Sharon Newman*

Wyoming Valley Star, 67" x 85", © Sally Schneider, 1993.
Quilted by Kari Lane.

That Patchwork Place • PO Box 118 • Bothell, WA 98041-0118

*From **ScrapMania** by Sally Schneider*

Wyoming Valley Star, 67" x 85", © Sally Schneider, 1993.
Quilted by Kari Lane.

That Patchwork Place • PO Box 118 • Bothell, WA 98041-0118

From **ScrapMania** *by Sally Schneider*

Autumn Botanica, 73" x 88",
© Laura Munson Reinstatler, 1993.

That Patchwork Place • PO Box 118 • Bothell, WA 98041-0118

*From **Botanical Wreaths: Nature's Glory in Appliqué***
by Laura Munson Reinstatler

Autumn Botanica, 73" x 88",
© Laura Munson Reinstatler, 1993.

That Patchwork Place • PO Box 118 • Bothell, WA 98041-0118

*From **Botanical Wreaths: Nature's Glory in Appliqué***
by Laura Munson Reinstatler

Through the Year with Sunbonnet Sue Two, 68" x 84",
© Sue Linker, 1990.

That Patchwork Place • PO Box 118 • Bothell, WA 98041-0118

*From **Sunbonnet Sue All Through the Year** by Sue Linker*

Through the Year with Sunbonnet Sue Two, 68" x 84",
© Sue Linker, 1990.

That Patchwork Place • PO Box 118 • Bothell, WA 98041-0118

From **Sunbonnet Sue All Through the Year** *by Sue Linker*

McSlusser's Garden, 36" x 44",
© Donna Ingram Slusser, 1994.

That Patchwork Place • PO Box 118 • Bothell, WA 98041-0118

From **Round Robin Quilts: Friendship Quilts of the '90s
and Beyond** *by Pat Maixner Magaret and Donna Ingram Slusser*

McSlusser's Garden, 36" x 44",
© Donna Ingram Slusser, 1994.

That Patchwork Place • PO Box 118 • Bothell, WA 98041-0118

From **Round Robin Quilts: Friendship Quilts of the '90s
and Beyond** *by Pat Maixner Magaret and Donna Ingram Slusser*

Christmas Star, 53³/₄" x 67¹/₄", © Judy Dafoe Hopkins, 1995. Quilted by Mrs. Emma Smucker.

That Patchwork Place • PO Box 118 • Bothell, WA 98041-0118

*From **Down the Rotary Road with Judy Hopkins***

Christmas Star, 53³/₄" x 67¹/₄", © Judy Dafoe Hopkins, 1995. Quilted by Mrs. Emma Smucker.

That Patchwork Place • PO Box 118 • Bothell, WA 98041-0118

*From **Down the Rotary Road with Judy Hopkins***

In Bloom, 61" x 82", © Gabrielle Swain, 1994.

That Patchwork Place • PO Box 118 • Bothell, WA 98041-0118

*From **Appliqué in Bloom** by Gabrielle Swain*

In Bloom, 61" x 82", © Gabrielle Swain, 1994.

That Patchwork Place • PO Box 118 • Bothell, WA 98041-0118

*From **Appliqué in Bloom** by Gabrielle Swain*

Friendship Star, 34" x 52", © Nancy J. Martin, 1994.
Quilted by Donna K. Gundlach.

That Patchwork Place • PO Box 118 • Bothell, WA 98041-0118

*From **Simply Scrappy Quilts** by Nancy J. Martin*

Friendship Star, 34" x 52", © Nancy J. Martin, 1994.
Quilted by Donna K. Gundlach.

That Patchwork Place • PO Box 118 • Bothell, WA 98041-0118

*From **Simply Scrappy Quilts** by Nancy J. Martin*

Shoo Fly Star, 56" x 72", © Nancy J. Martin, 1996.
Quilted by Amanda Miller's quilters.

That Patchwork Place • PO Box 118 • Bothell, WA 98041-0118

*Pattern from **Rotary Roundup** by Judy Dafoe Hopkins
and Nancy J. Martin*

Shoo Fly Star, 56" x 72", © Nancy J. Martin, 1996.
Quilted by Amanda Miller's quilters.

That Patchwork Place • PO Box 118 • Bothell, WA 98041-0118

*Pattern from **Rotary Roundup** by Judy Dafoe Hopkins and Nancy J. Martin*

In the Land of Little Quilts, 44" x 54", © Little Quilts, 1995.

That Patchwork Place • PO Box 118 • Bothell, WA 98041-0118

*From **Celebrating the Quilt: Twenty Quilts for Twenty Years**
by That Patchwork Place*

In the Land of Little Quilts, 44" x 54", © Little Quilts, 1995.

That Patchwork Place • PO Box 118 • Bothell, WA 98041-0118

From **Celebrating the Quilt: Twenty Quilts for Twenty Years**
by That Patchwork Place

Rose Red, 60" x 60", © Sheila Wintle, 1993.

That Patchwork Place • PO Box 118 • Bothell, WA 98041-0118

*From **Class-Act Quilts: 18 Eclectic Quilts by Teachers and Their Students** by That Patchwork Place*

Rose Red, 60" x 60", © Sheila Wintle, 1993.

That Patchwork Place • PO Box 118 • Bothell, WA 98041-0118

*From **Class-Act Quilts: 18 Eclectic Quilts by Teachers and Their Students** by That Patchwork Place*